# BEAUTIFUL GROWTH

## 40 Days of Prayer

# Beautiful Growth:
# 40 Days of Prayer

My mind sometimes wanders when I try to pray. That is why I started writing prayers. When my pen is moving, I am able to focus better. I know that I need to learn to be still and quiet in my time with God, but I am the first to tell you that I am a work in progress. I am thankful that we serve a loving and patient God.

While I am sharing areas where I need to grow, I will go ahead and confess that I am not skilled at memorizing scripture. This was another factor that motivated me to write this book. When I write my prayer praying back God's Word to him, it helps me learn scripture.

I wrote most of these prayers without knowing what I would title this book. As I proofread the prayers, I saw several where I requested that God would help me grow in certain areas. Growth can be painful. It can involve change and so many of us are not fans of change. When I reflect back on seasons of change and growth, I see God's hand in it, and I know that there is beauty in growth.

As you read these prayers and scriptures, I pray that you will be inspired to write your own prayers and dig deeper into the Word.

Thank you for allowing me to be part of your prayer journey. May it be a time of beautiful growth.

Dear Lord,

<u>Thank you for making us new</u>. Help us grow closer to you each and every day. We know that as we reach out to you in prayer and read your Word, you will grow us. We know that as that occurs there may be growing pains, but we also know that there is beauty in growth. I pray that we may be disciplined to focus on you and to quiet the noise of our day enough to truly hear you. Amen.

Therefore, if anyone is in Christ,
the new creation has come. The
old has gone, the new is here!
2 Corinthians 5:17

Dear Lord,

I pray that your peace will be with me during the busy seasons of life.  There seems to be several of those seasons thus far.  I know that you have a plan, and it is a good one.  Remind me of that when my thoughts stray and worries try to creep in.  <u>You work all things for the good of those that love you</u>.  Let me feel that deep in my soul and not doubt.  Amen.

And we know that in all things
God works for the good of those
who love him, who have been
called according to his purpose.
Romans 8:28

Dear Lord,

As I approached these last couple of days, I felt a peace that is only explained by you. There were more tasks than should have been possible. I needed to be more places than I physically could at one time. Thank you for your patience in the moments that we get frazzled, and thank you for the reassurance that you are good and your love endures forever. You are faithful to us and will continue to be faithful to your family of believers through all generations. Amen.

His goodness endures forever.

For the Lord is good and his love
endure forever; his faithfulness
continues through all generations.
Psalms 100:5

Dear Lord,

There is much to be excited about and focus on in this life. I am thankful for the opportunities that you have given us. Please help me to remember that all of "this" is temporary, and you are not. <u>You will not be shaken</u>. I am amazed at your strength. Help me to remember to lean into you when I am weary. <u>You will take on my worries and sustain me</u> and carry me when I can go no further. You will never let me fall so far that you will not be there to pick me back up. Thank you. Amen.

Therefore, since we are receiving a
kingdom that cannot be shaken, let us
be thankful, and so worship God
acceptably with reverence and awe, for
our "God is a consuming fire."
Hebrews 12:28-29

Cast your cares on the Lord
and he will sustain you;
he will never let
the righteous be shaken.  Psalms 55:22

Dear Lord,
I know that <u>worry will not add a moment to my life</u>, but in the back of mind it sometimes lurks. <u>If I ask, you will answer</u>. If I knock, a door will be opened. As I give my worries to you, help me also <u>to confess my shortcomings to my friends, so that they may pray me through them</u> as well. <u>Please remove my anxiousness and gently remind me to turn to you in prayer and petition</u> with a thankful and trusting heart. Amen.

"Can any one of you by worrying add a single hour to your life?"
Matthew 6:27

Therefore confess your sins to each other and pray for each other so that you may be healed. The prayer of a righteous person is powerful and effective. James 5:16

Do not be anxious about anything, but in every situation, by prayer and petition, with thanksgiving, present your requests to God. Philippians 4:6

Dear Lord,
You do not hold onto the past,
so why do I?  Why do I want to
recount my wrongs when you
have already wiped my slate
clean?  <u>You keep no record</u>, no
tally marks.  You offer full
forgiveness when we ask and
repent.  Help me to "let go & let
God".  Let me give it to you and
not look back so that my focus
can be forward on you and on
how I can better serve you.
  Amen.

Let go &
let God.

If you, Lord, kept a record of sins,
Lord, who could stand?
But with you there is forgiveness,
so that we can, with reverence, serve
you.
Psalms 130: 3-4

Dear Lord,

When I think about it, it is hard to comprehend how you can listen to me and speak to me and to all others communicating with you at the same time! I have trouble focusing with communication just within my family, but you are God and I am not! You are amazing in ways that it is perfectly okay for me to not be able to understand. Thank you for always listening to me and for sending <u>the Holy Spirit to help guide me into all the truth</u>.

Amen.

But when he, the Spirit of truth, comes, he will guide you into all the truth. He will not speak on his own; he will speak only what he hears, and he will tell you what is yet to come. John 16:13

*Let us have ears to hear you.* ♥

Dear Lord,
I pray that you will help us navigate away from and not let us move towards things that tempt us. We know that the temptations to stray from you are not from you but from ourselves, from our own evil desires. Thank you for your Word. Help us to treasure it and store it in our hearts so that we may not stray away from you but grow even closer instead.
Amen.

the WORD

I have hidden your word in my heart
that I might not sin against you.
Psalms 119:11

Dear Lord,

Life is a bit crazy, especially when we try to "do life" without you. That is why today we want to pause and thank you for your instructions on peace and your promises to us. Help us <u>to seek peace if at all possible to the best of our abilities</u> and to draw strength from you and guidance from you when it exceeds our abilities. When that does happen, we are so thankful to know that we are not alone. <u>You are near to us always</u>. All we must do is call out, reach out, and you will answer. Thank you Lord. Amen.

The LORD is near to all who call on him,
to all who call on him in truth.
Psalms 145:18

If it is possible, as far as it depends on
you, live at peace with everyone.
Romans 12:18

Dear Lord,
There is no "storm" we cannot survive as long as our faith is in Jesus. We know that <u>he calmed the wind and waves in the boat</u>, and he can and will calm the storms in our lives too. Help us to remember that he gave us the Holy Spirit to guide us, comfort us, calm us and communicate for us when we cannot manage. Thank you for <u>your amazing grace being sufficient and for your power being made perfect when we are weak</u>. These promises sustain us.  Amen.

But he said to me, "My grace is sufficient for you, for my power is made perfect in weakness." Therefore I will boast all the more gladly about my weaknesses, so that Christ's power may rest on me.
2 Corinthians 12:9

The disciples went and woke him, saying, "Lord, save us! We're going to drown!" He replied, "You of little faith, why are you so afraid? "Then he got up and rebuked the winds and the waves, and it was completely calm. The men were amazed and asked, "What kind of man is this? Even the winds and the waves obey him!" Matthew 8:25-27

Dear Lord,
You know that we are tired. When we feel this way it is easy to sink into despair, but you promise to renew us and give us strength. You do allow us to go through times of trouble, of discomfort, but this is not to punish us. These times are to grow us and show us your ways and your love; we receive compassion from you and learn how to comfort others in their time of need. Thank you for being a patient teacher and father. Amen.

Praise be to the God and Father of our Lord Jesus Christ, the Father of compassion and the God of all comfort.  2 Corinthians 1:3

"I will refresh the weary and satisfy the faint." Jeremiah 31:25

Dear Lord,

Springtime makes me smile. I love to see new growth -- the buds on the trees & the plants sprouting green in the brown dirt. We are like those plants. We have seasons of growth. Sometimes the growth is visible. Sometimes you are working on us in ways that are not seen. Help me to remember that in all seasons of life <u>you are here to guide us, to satisfy our needs & give us strength</u>. We are thankful for the blooms in life & for the times that we rest & grow our roots deeper into you. Amen.

The Lord will guide you always;
he will satisfy your needs in a sun-
scorched land and will strengthen
your frame. You will be like a well-
watered garden, like a spring whose
waters never fail.
Isaiah 58:11

Dear Lord,
We are tired. We are not physically tired. We are emotionally tired. Things happen in life that make no sense to our human minds, but even as we struggle we desire to look ahead, to fix our gaze on you. We know that we can do all things through you who gives us strength -- strength and rest. We seek that rest now. Please let us bring our burdens to you and find rest in your love. Amen.

"Come to me, all you who are weary and burdened, and I will give you rest."  Matthew 11:28

Let your eyes look straight ahead; fix your gaze directly before you. Proverbs 4:25

I can do all this through him who gives me strength.  Philippians 4:13

Dear Lord,
 We know that we do not deserve all that you do for us, but we are thankful. You do not have a point system for us to earn your love. You give it freely, and you gave your son for us while we were still sinners. How amazing is that love! We pray that you will work in us and help us to share your beautiful love with others. Let us be a light to all.  May they see your love in our words and actions. Amen.

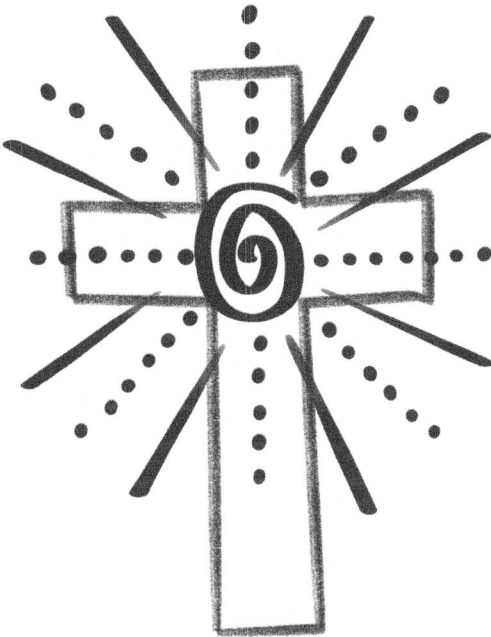

But God demonstrates his own love for us in this: While we were still sinners, Christ died for us.  Romans 5:8

Dear Lord,

I am always amazed at how great your love is for us. It is immeasurable and hard to grasp the fullness of it sometimes. <u>You gave your son to save us. He endured beatings and the cross to save us from ourselves. He took our sins to heal us</u>. He became broken to make us whole. I pray that when we feel unloved or unworthy that you will help us to remember you love us this much--enough to die for us. Thank you Lord. Amen.

But he was pierced for our
transgressions, he was crushed for our
iniquities; the punishment that brought
us peace was on him, and by his wounds
we are healed.  Isaiah 53:5

Dear Lord,

Today I am asking that you help us pin point what in our life pulls us from you. Help us clearly see what distracts us. As we discover what takes our focus off of you, help us evaluate what is important. I pray that we may refocus and know that you come first. Let us declutter our thoughts and give you room, room to guide us, <u>to help us find rest in you and to give us hope. Please let us be still</u> and quiet long enough to hear you and to be reminded that <u>you are our God</u>. Amen.

# be still
## and KNOW

Yes, my soul, find rest in God; my hope comes from him.  Psalms 62:5

He says, "Be still, and know that I am God; I will be exalted among the nations, I will be exalted in the earth." Psalms 46:10

Dear Lord,
We are so thankful that you know our needs especially when we cannot figure them out ourselves! We need each other. We need friends <u>to encourage us and motivate us to acts of love and good works</u>. <u>Let us not neglect meeting together</u>. You know that we need a community to hold us accountable and to push us when we need that extra nudge. Thank you for those in our life who get in our space even when we may not think we want them in there.
  Amen.

Let us think of ways to motivate one another to acts of love and good works.  And let us not neglect our meeting together, as some people do, but encourage one another, especially now that the day of his return is drawing near.
Hebrews 10: 24-25

Dear Lord,

There are times that we feel down even when all is right in our world. Sometimes sadness gets the best of us. We must remember that you have overcome it all, and you did it for us. <u>You chose us before creation began</u>. I pray that whatever weighs us down may be lifted up from our hearts and our shoulders as we revel in your love and remember that <u>we are chosen</u> and loved so very much by you. Amen.

For he chose us in him before the creation of the world to be holy and blameless in his sight.
Ephesians 1:4

you are
CHOSEN

Dear Lord,

I am not perfect. None of us are perfect. I can get caught up in my flaws, or I can choose to remember that I am your creation.  <u>I am fearfully and wonderfully made</u> by you.  You do not expect me to be perfect, but you love me just the way I am, the way you created me to be.  May my heart be open to hear you guide me each day to walk in the path that you would have me take. Please let my focus not be on my imperfections but on how I can grow in my faith and love you more daily.  Amen.

I praise you because I am fearfully
and wonderfully made;
your works are wonderful,
I know that full well.
Psalms 139:14

YOU are
fearfully &
wonderfully made.

Dear Lord,

We find ourselves in a hole sometimes.  It may even be one that we dug for ourselves!  Help us not to stay stuck in it.  Let us remember that if we will keep at it, if we will keep the faith, _that in your time we will reap the harvest of blessings_ that you have in store for each one of us. _May we not get tired of doing good_.  Don't let us look down into the "hole", but may our eyes be open and looking up towards you and for opportunities where we can help others.  Amen.

So let's not get tired of doing what is good. At just the right time we will reap a harvest of blessing if we don't give up.  Therefore, whenever we have the opportunity, we should do good to everyone—especially to those in the family of faith.
Galatians 6:9-10

be the
GOOD

Dear Lord,
Your love for us is so amazing. It is grand to the point that it is hard to grasp at times.  There are valleys in life where we feel unloved or unworthy. May those thoughts and feelings be fleeting.  Don't let us wallow in them, but let us look up to you and remember our worth.  We know that your love for us knows no bounds. <u>You loved us so much that you gave your one and only Son, so that we may have eternal life with you</u>.  That is the only reason we need to know that we are worthy, and we are loved by you.  Amen.

For God so loved the world that he gave his one and only Son, that whoever believes in him shall not perish but have eternal life.  For God did not send his Son into the world to condemn the world, but to save the world through him.
John 3:16-17

Dear Lord,
We thank you for your guidance.  It is a beautiful blessing to have your written word readily available.  My day is so different when I start it feasting on your word.  Some days don't start that way, and later I will wonder what is wrong.  The answer is pretty simple.  Your command is clear. We are to love you with all our heart, all our soul and all our mind.  Help me to remember my priorities and know that you long to be first.  Amen.

When your words turned up, I feasted on them; and they became my joy, the delight of my heart, because I belong to you, LORD God of heavenly forces.  Jeremiah 15:16

Jesus replied, "You must love the Lord your God with all your hear, all your soul, and all your mind."
Matthew 22:37

Dear Lord,
I do not want to be known as a follower of this world and its trends but as a follower of you. I pray that as I read your word I will be able to discern more and more about your good, pleasing and perfect will for me. I do seek to do your will even when it goes against the norm of the day. I want my thoughts to be pleasing to you and my actions to show others my love for you.
Amen.

Do not conform to the pattern of this world, but be transformed by the renewing of your mind.  Then you will be able to test and approve what God's will is -- his good, pleasing and perfect will.
Romans 12:2

Dear Lord,

May I grow in my faith day by day. I am tempted at times to doubt <u>that which is not visible</u>, but I know that is what faith is about. <u>Faith is trusting you and in your creations and your promises without seeing</u>. Thank you for being patient with me when my faith is weak. <u>I do believe you exist and that you reward those who earnestly seek you</u>. I know that you are there waiting on me and nudging me at times to remember your goodness.

Amen.

# faith

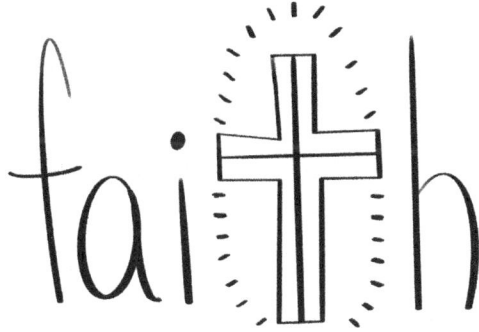

By faith we understand that the universe was formed at God's command, so that what is seen was not made out of what was visible.
Hebrews 11:3

And without faith it is impossible to please God, because anyone who comes to him must believe that he exists and that he rewards those who earnestly seek him.
Hebrews 11:6

Dear Lord,

You are my helper. <u>You are my strength</u>. I may stumble at times, but when I refocus and <u>put my eyes on you</u> I know that you will be a steady hand to hold me up and <u>not let me be shaken</u>. This gives me such comfort. The joy I feel from having your peace puts a smile on my face and in my heart. I pray that you know how thankful I am to have a relationship with you. I know that <u>I can trust you with all my heart</u> and what a blessing that is! Amen.

# Always be thankful ♥

The LORD is my strength and my shield, I trust him with all my heart. He helps me, and my heart is filled with joy.  I burst out in songs of thanksgiving.  Psalms 28:7

I keep my eyes always on the Lord. With him at my right hand, I will not be shaken.  Psalms 16:8

Dear Lord,
When others look at us we want them to see your love. We want our hands to do acts that show others how you care. We want our smile to be warm and show your kindness. We want our actions to be more like those of Jesus and less like what the ways of this world look like. <u>We want to shine before others that they may see your good deeds and glorify you</u>. Please open our eyes to opportunities to do so and give us the strength to do it even when it is not the popular or easy thing to do. Amen.

be the light

"You are the light of the world. A town built on a hill cannot be hidden. Neither do people light a lamp and put it under a bowl. Instead they put it on a stand, and it gives light to everyone in the house. In the same way, let your light shine before others that they may see your good deeds and glorify your Father in heaven."
Matthew 5:14-16

Dear Lord,

I want to be like Mary.  I want to believe and to trust you wholeheartedly.  Mary believed your words even when they made no sense to her.  She did not doubt you.  I pray that my ears may be open to hear you, my eyes open to see you and my heart open to love you.  As I hear you, may I truly listen and trust and believe.  I no longer want to be a doubter.  Please help me to grow in my relationship with you and <u>to believe that you will fulfill your promises</u>.  Amen.

Blessed is she who has believed
that the Lord would fulfill his
promises to her!  Luke 1:45

Dear Lord,
We know that we have worldly responsibilities. There are daily, weekly, monthly tasks that simply have to be done. We fail you when we let these activities take priority over you. Please help us to put you first, always. When we do this, <u>we have chosen the better part</u>. When we do this, you are in our hearts and minds and guide our actions. And in this way, all will be well. Amen.

"Martha, Martha," the Lord answered, "you are worried and upset and about many things, but few things are needed -- or indeed only one. Mary has chosen what is better, and it will not be taken away from her." Luke 10:41-42

Dear Lord,
What direction do you want us to go Lord? How do you want to use us?  Help us to discover our gifts so that we can use them in ways that shows others your love and promises. You know that we want to do "it" our way sometimes, but we do know that your way is so much better. <u>We want to follow you and not go our own way</u>.  Please guide us back to you when we wander off.  Sometimes we need a nudge...or a push.  Thank you for providing both.  Amen.

Then he said to the crowd, "If any of you wants to be my follower, you must give up your own way, take up your cross daily, and follow me."
Luke 9:23

Dear Lord,

Oh, how comforting to know that I am never alone. <u>You are working in me</u>, with me, for me! What are you encouraging me to do? We earnestly seek to follow the path that you would have us take.  I know that you have a plan, and I know that your plan is good. I pray that we may be still enough and quiet enough to know your will and then be obedient <u>to do that which will please you</u>.  Amen.

For God is working in you, giving you the desire and the power to do what pleases him.  Philippians 2:13

Dear Lord,

When we accepted you, you sent the Holy Spirit to live within us. Some days I am better at acknowledging the presence of the Holy Spirit than others. I pray that I may live by the Spirit daily and that my whole being may be attuned to you. I want to be open to your leading in every part of my life -- not just select areas that are easy. Please open my heart to your guidance and help me to follow you. Amen.

Since we are living by the Spirit, let us follow the Spirit's leading in every part of our lives.
Galatians 5:25

# Lord

## lead me ♡

Dear Lord,

Thank you for this day. It is a present! When I let the troubles of tomorrow or next week or next month cloud my thoughts, please let me remember <u>each day has enough trouble of its own</u> without me looking beyond for more. While some days certainly go smoother than others, each can have joy found in it when our source of joy is you. <u>Teach us to number our days, that we may gain a heart of wisdom</u>. Thank you Lord for gifting us another day. Amen.

Therefore do no worry about tomorrow, for tomorrow will worry about itself. Each day has enough trouble of its own. Matthew 6:34

Teach us to number our days, that we may gain a heart of wisdom. Psalms 90:12

Dear Lord,
I am thankful for the many relationships in my life. We need you, and we need others. We need friends to celebrate with when life is exciting and <u>to pick us up when life is hard</u>. Isolating ourselves may seem like the best answer. We think that we are no good to anyone. You know better. It is not good for us to fly solo in this life. You said yourself <u>that it is not good for man to be alone</u>. Thank you for always being there for us and for putting those people in our life that love you and love us too. Amen.

The Lord God said, "It is not good for the man to be alone. I will make a helper suitable for him."
Genesis 2:18

If either of them falls down, one can help the other up. But pity anyone who falls and has no one to help them up.  Ecclesiastes 4:10

Dear Lord,
We often doubt our value, our self worth. We base our value on what we have accomplished at work or how we look or what we drive. None of these temporary things matter to you. We know that you loved and valued us while we were being created before we even took our first breath. <u>We are your masterpiece, and you have wonderful plans for each one of us</u>. Please help us to know that our worth is found in you alone. Amen.

For we are God's masterpiece. He has created us anew in Christ Jesus, so that we can do the good things he planned for us long ago.
Ephesians 2:10

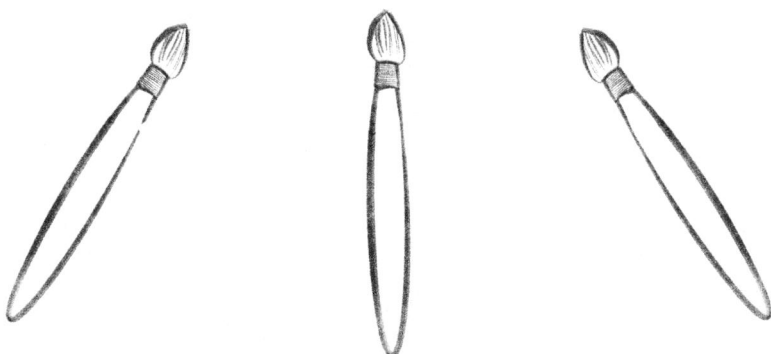

Dear Lord,
Please guide us to bear good fruit! We know that we cannot produce the fruit of the Spirit by our own power or methods. <u>We must follow the lead of your Holy Spirit and let it be our guide in every area of our life</u>, not just our spiritual part. You want to be our go-to, our guide, our leader and our friend. Help us to not section you off into only Sunday morning or Wednesday night, but let us have your Spirit fill us 24/7. May we be spirit filled fruit bearers showing this world your love. Amen.

Those who belong to Christ Jesus have nailed the passions and desires of their sinful nature to his cross and crucified them there.  If we are living by the Holy Spirit, let us follow the Holy Spirit's leading in every part of our lives.
Galatians 5:24-25

Dear Lord,
A dear friend has told me many times that life is made of peaks and valleys.  She has encouraged me to find joy in both and not to rush through life wishing time away.  There is <u>joy in your presence</u> and peace to be found in all situations when we rely on you.  Thank you for friends who help us seek joy on our journey.  <u>May we always be joyful, pray continually and give thanks for whatever happens</u>.  We know that this is what you want for us.  Amen.

You have made known to me the paths of life; you fill me with joy in your presence.  Acts 2:28

Always be joyful.  Pray continually, and give thanks whatever happens. That is what God wants for you in Christ Jesus.
1 Thessalonians 5:16-18

JOY

♥ -in my soul- ♥
♥ -because of Him- ♥

Dear Lord,

Why do we worry?  We know better!  You do give us this character trait because it can be used as a warning sign alerting us that we need to be aware of a situation.  BUT, you do not intend for us to sit in it.  Worry without action is draining and <u>will not add a single hour to our life</u>.  It does nothing positive for us, and <u>it weighs us down</u>.  Help us give our worries to you in prayer, and <u>let us be an encourager to others</u> in their time of worry.  Amen.

Worry weighs a person down; an encouraging word cheers a person up.  Proverbs 12:25

"Can anyone of you by worrying add a single hour to your life?"
Matthew 6:27

Dear Lord,
You are an amazing artist.  Not many things make me pause and be so aware of you more than a beautiful sunrise.  The colors you paint the sky with are so vibrant.  <u>They proclaim the work of your hands</u>.  I do not know how someone can see a sunrise and not think of you.  <u>Your invisible qualities are made visible in nature and creation</u>.  Thank you for reminders in nature all around us showing us your handiwork.  May we have eyes to see them. Amen.

The heavens declare the glory of God; the skies proclaim the work of his hands.  Psalms 19:1

For since the creation of the world God's invisible qualities -- his eternal power and divine nature -- have been clearly seen, being understood from what has been made, so that people are without excuse.  Romans 1:20

Dear Lord,
Thank you for reminding us that there is beauty in the ordinary.
We can get caught up in the excitement of new things and in searching for the next best thing to come into our lives.
YOU are the best thing.
Period. Blessings from you are all around for us to see when we take time to look around instead of down at our phone or up ahead at what is coming next.
Help us to see the blessings in our ordinary daily life, to feel contentment in our soul and to know that you are all we truly need. Amen.

Yet true godliness with contentment is itself great wealth. After all, we brought nothing with us when we came into the world, and we can't take anything with us when we leave it.  So if we have enough food and clothing, let us be content.  1 Timothy 6:6-8

Dear Lord,
We are thankful for the people that you have placed in our lives.  Sometimes we want to shut ourselves off from the world, from our people, but that is not what you want us to do.  We need you first, but we also need others.  <u>Two are better off than one</u>.  We hold each other accountable, <u>we sharpen one another</u> and we encourage each other when we are in a hole. We were made for community. If we have not found a community where we can thrive, please show us the way there. Amen.

Two people are better off than one, for they can help each other succeed. If one person falls, the other can reach out and help. But someone who falls alone is in real trouble.  Ecclesiastes 4:9-10

As iron sharpens iron, so a friends sharpens a friend.  Proverbs 27:17

Thank you so much for letting me be a part of your prayer life. I pray that you have seen growth in your spiritual life and in your relationship with God.

If you would like to find other journals and devotionals by myself and my fellow JoySeeker, Jennifer Bridges, we can be found at:

www.joyseekers.net

joy.seekers

www.facebook.com/joyseekers2